Alexander Arthur Van Halen: The Rhythmic Force Behind Van Halen

Born on May 8, 1953, in Amsterdam, Alexander Arthur Van Halen, better known as Alex Van Halen, grew up surrounded by music. The son of Jan van Halen, a talented jazz saxophonist and clarinetist, and Eugenia van Beers, an Indo woman from the Dutch East Indies, Alex's early years were steeped in rich cultural influences. His family lived in Nijmegen, in the Netherlands, before moving to Pasadena, California, in 1962, where Alex and his younger brother Eddie became naturalized U.S. citizens.

Both brothers were classically trained pianists, but Alex's musical journey took an unexpected turn when he picked up Eddie's drum kit. What began as casual practice soon turned into a passion, and by the time he mastered the drum solo from The Surfaris' "Wipe Out," it was clear that drumming was his true calling. Eddie, recognizing his brother's talent, switched from drums to guitar, setting the stage for one of the most legendary partnerships in rock history.

In their early teens, the Van Halen brothers formed their first band, "The Broken Combs," performing at lunchtime at Hamilton Elementary School in Pasadena. This was just the beginning of their musical exploration. After graduating from Pasadena High School in 1971, Alex briefly studied music theory at Pasadena City College, where he met future bandmates Michael Anthony and David Lee Roth. Together, they formed the band Mammoth, which would later be renamed Van Halen in 1974.

Van Halen's rise to fame was meteoric. After signing with Warner Bros. in 1977, the band released their self-titled debut album in 1978. It was a groundbreaking success, setting the tone for their iconic sound and influencing countless musicians. Over the years, Van Halen released twelve studio albums, with Alex and Eddie being the only constant members throughout the band's storied career.

Known for his powerful and intricate drumming, Alex developed what he called the "brown sound"—a deep, rich tone that became a signature of his snare drum. His influence in the rock world was immense, with drummers like John Bonham and Keith Moon serving as inspirations, while Alex's own style left an indelible mark on the genre.

Despite his success, Alex never recorded music without his brother Eddie. The bond between them was more than just familial; it was the foundation of Van Halen's sound. The only time Alex stepped outside this dynamic was for the track "Respect the Wind," which he co-wrote and performed with Eddie for the 1996 movie Twister. This piece earned the brothers a Grammy nomination for Best Rock Instrumental Performance.

Alex's personal life was marked by both challenges and joys. He married Valeri Kendall in 1983, but the marriage ended after just two months. His second marriage, to Kelly Carter in 1984, resulted in the birth of his son Aric in 1989, but the couple divorced in 1996. In 2000, Alex found lasting happiness with his third wife, Stine Schyberg, with whom he has a son named Malcolm.

Beyond music, Alex's life took on a spiritual dimension. He became an ordained minister and officiated at his brother Eddie's second wedding in 2009, as well as at the wedding of Valerie Bertinelli, his former sister-in-law, in 2011.

However, years of loud music took a toll on Alex's hearing. In 1995, he began using custom in-ear monitors to protect his hearing while performing on stage. Despite these challenges, his passion for music never waned.

Following Eddie's death in 2020, Van Halen disbanded, marking the end of an era. In June 2024, Alex auctioned off his drum gear, signaling that his time in the spotlight might have come to an end. Yet, his legacy continues, not just through the music he created but also through his forthcoming book, Brothers, set to be released in October 2024.

Alex Van Halen's story is one of dedication, innovation, and an unbreakable bond with his brother Eddie, together creating a musical legacy that will resonate for generations to come.

4o

Though the drums may have fallen silent, Alex Van Halen's impact on rock music endures. The announcement of his book, Brothers, has sparked significant interest among fans and musicians alike. Set to be released in October 2024, the memoir is expected to offer a deeply personal account of his life, focusing on his relationship with Eddie and the journey they shared as co-founders of one of the most influential rock bands in history.

Alex's story is not just one of musical achievement but also of resilience and evolution. His early years in the Netherlands, his move to America, and the challenges of adapting to a new culture all played a role in shaping his identity. The bond he shared with Eddie was more than just that of brothers; it was a creative partnership that defined their lives. Together, they navigated the highs and lows of fame, from the exhilaration of performing in sold-out arenas to the personal struggles that accompanied life in the spotlight.

Despite the pressures of fame, Alex remained grounded, a testament to his strong family ties and the cultural values instilled in him by his parents. His Dutch heritage and his mother's Indonesian roots gave him a unique perspective, influencing not just his music but also his approach to life. This cultural richness, combined with his classical training, made him a drummer who could seamlessly blend technical skill with raw power, creating a sound that was both innovative and timeless.

Alex's contributions to Van Halen were not limited to his drumming. He was also deeply involved in the band's management, often taking on roles behind the scenes to ensure their success. Whether it was booking gigs in their early days or making critical decisions about the band's direction, Alex's influence was felt in every aspect of Van Halen's operations. His leadership, combined with Eddie's musical genius, made them a formidable team, one that revolutionized rock music.

As the years passed, Alex continued to push the boundaries of what was possible on the drums. His use of extravagant drum kits, complete with orchestral gongs and multiple bass drums, became a hallmark of Van Halen's live performances. He wasn't just playing the drums; he was creating a visual and auditory spectacle that captivated audiences around the world. His signature sound, particularly the "brown sound" of his snare drum, became a defining element of Van Halen's music, influencing countless drummers who followed in his footsteps.

In his personal life, Alex faced both triumphs and challenges. His short-lived first marriage was followed by a more stable union with Kelly Carter, with whom he had his first son, Aric. Though this marriage also ended in divorce, it was during this time that Alex began to explore other aspects of his identity, including his spirituality. Becoming an ordained minister allowed him to connect with his family in a new way, particularly when he officiated at Eddie's wedding and at Valerie Bertinelli's second marriage.

The birth of his second son, Malcolm, with his third wife, Stine Schyberg, brought new joy into Alex's life. Despite the pressures of his career and the demands of fame, Alex remained a dedicated father, supporting his children in their pursuits. His son Aric's passion for running, which led him to compete in the Olympic trials for the steeplechase in 2016, was a source of immense pride for Alex, who understood the importance of pursuing one's passions.

As Van Halen's music continued to inspire new generations, Alex's legacy as a drummer and musician became firmly cemented in rock history. Even after the band's disbandment following Eddie's death, Alex's influence remained strong. The decision to auction off his drum gear in 2024 was a poignant moment, signaling the end of an era, but it also underscored Alex's understanding that his musical journey was inextricably linked to his brother's presence.

The upcoming release of Brothers is expected to provide fans with an intimate look at the man behind the drums, offering insights into his relationship with Eddie, his experiences in the music industry, and the personal moments that shaped his life. For Alex Van Halen, the story is not just about the music; it's about the bond between brothers, the journey of self-discovery, and the legacy that lives on through the beats he laid down and the music that continues to resonate long after the final note has been played.

As Alex steps away from the stage, his story serves as a reminder of the enduring power of music and the unbreakable bond between family. His journey, marked by innovation, perseverance, and a deep love for his craft, will continue to inspire musicians and fans alike for generations to come.

As Alex Van Halen transitions into this new chapter of his life, away from the bright lights and roaring crowds, his legacy remains deeply woven into the fabric of rock and roll. The story of Van Halen is not just about the rise of one of the most iconic bands in history; it's about the evolution of a genre, the pushing of musical boundaries, and the creation of a sound that defined an era.

Reflecting on his journey, Alex often acknowledges the role his brother Eddie played in his life, both as a musical partner and as a confidant. Their dynamic was unique—a relationship built on mutual respect and an unspoken understanding that transcended words. Together, they crafted some of the most memorable riffs and rhythms in rock music, with Alex's drumming providing the powerful, steady backbone to Eddie's virtuosic guitar work. Their synergy was palpable, and it became the cornerstone of Van Halen's success.

Even as the band reached the pinnacle of success, Alex never lost sight of the values his parents instilled in him. Jan and Eugenia van Halen's emphasis on discipline, hard work, and the importance of family left a lasting impression on Alex and Eddie. The lessons learned from their father's jazz background and their mother's rich cultural heritage were evident in the brothers' approach to music and life. The blend of classical training with a passion for rock and roll set the Van Halen brothers apart from their peers, making them true pioneers in their field.

Throughout Van Halen's storied career, Alex's drumming evolved alongside the band's sound. From the raw, energetic beats of their early albums to the more refined and experimental rhythms of later records, Alex continuously pushed himself to explore new techniques and sounds. His work on tracks like "Hot for Teacher," with its iconic double-bass drumming, and "Everybody Wants Some!!" showcased his technical prowess and creativity. These performances not only elevated the band's music but also cemented Alex's reputation as one of the most influential drummers in rock history.

The bond between Alex and Eddie wasn't just professional; it was deeply personal. They shared a connection that was almost telepathic, especially when they were on stage. The energy they fed off each other was electric, creating performances that were as much about the interaction between the two brothers as they were about the music itself. Fans could feel the chemistry between them, and it became a defining feature of Van Halen's live shows.

When Eddie passed away in 2020, the loss was immeasurable for Alex. It marked the end of an era, not just for the band, but for Alex as a musician. Eddie wasn't just his brother; he was his partner in every sense of the word. The decision to disband Van Halen shortly after Eddie's death was a testament to the depth of their relationship. For Alex, there was no Van Halen without Eddie.

As he steps into the role of author with his memoir, Brothers, Alex is offering fans a rare glimpse into the personal side of his life and career. The book is expected to delve into the highs and lows of their journey—from their early days as immigrant children in California to their rise to rock stardom, and the personal challenges they faced along the way. It will likely explore the complexities of their relationship, the sacrifices they made for their art, and the joy they found in creating music together.

In writing this memoir, Alex is not just preserving the legacy of Van Halen; he's paying tribute to the bond he shared with Eddie. It's a story of brotherhood, resilience, and the pursuit of a shared dream. For fans, Brothers will be more than just a behind-the-scenes look at one of rock's greatest bands; it will be an intimate portrait of two brothers who, despite the pressures of fame and the challenges they faced, remained united by their love for music and each other.

As Alex moves forward, his influence on music continues to be felt. Young drummers still study his techniques, and aspiring musicians look to Van Halen's body of work as a blueprint for success. The band's legacy lives on through the countless artists they've inspired and the enduring popularity of their music.

While Alex may have stepped away from performing, his contributions to the world of music are far from over. Whether through his upcoming book or his continued influence on the drumming community, Alex Van Halen's story is one of passion, innovation, and an unbreakable bond between brothers. It's a legacy that will endure, just like the thunderous beats that once echoed through arenas around the world.

As Alex Van Halen embraces the quieter moments of life away from the stage, he carries with him the echoes of a career that has left an indelible mark on the music industry. Yet, despite the immense success and the accolades that have followed, Alex remains grounded, anchored by the principles instilled in him from a young age.

His journey began in the vibrant streets of Amsterdam, where the sounds of his father's jazz music filled their home. Jan van Halen's dedication to his craft and the rich musical heritage passed down from his Dutch-Indonesian mother, Eugenia, laid the foundation for the Van Halen brothers' future. Moving to Pasadena, California, in 1962, the family faced the challenges of adapting to a new culture, but music was the constant that kept them connected to their roots and each other.

In Pasadena, the brothers' musical paths began to take shape, albeit in unexpected ways. Alex's initial foray into music was on the guitar, but fate had other plans. The sound of drums soon captured his imagination, and before long, Alex found himself behind the drum kit that Eddie had been saving up for. It was a serendipitous switch that would define their future, as Eddie turned his focus to the guitar, setting the stage for the legendary duo they would become.

Their early band, "The Broken Combs," was just the beginning. As they moved through different groups, refining their sound and honing their skills, it became clear that they were destined for something bigger. The formation of "Mammoth," and eventually the iconic Van Halen, was the culmination of years of hard work, experimentation, and a deep understanding of each other's musical strengths.

The decision to rename the band to Van Halen—a name that would become synonymous with rock royalty—was a pivotal moment. It marked the beginning of a new chapter, one that would see the brothers rise to the top of the rock world. Alex's drumming became the heartbeat of the band, his rhythms driving the music forward with an intensity and precision that few could match. Together with Eddie's groundbreaking guitar work, David Lee Roth's flamboyant vocals, and Michael Anthony's solid bass lines, Van Halen became a force to be reckoned with.

As the band's popularity soared, they quickly became known for their electrifying live performances. Alex's drumming was central to the energy of their shows, his powerful beats resonating with fans and leaving a lasting impression. The "brown sound" that he coined to describe the tone of his snare drum became a signature element of Van Halen's music, further cementing his role as a driving force behind the band's success.

Over the years, Van Halen's influence spread far and wide. Their debut album, released in 1978, was a game-changer, setting a new standard for hard rock and inspiring countless musicians. Album after album, the band pushed the boundaries of what rock music could be, blending technical skill with raw energy and a sense of fun that was infectious.

But behind the scenes, life wasn't always easy. The pressures of fame, the demands of constant touring, and personal challenges took their toll. Yet, through it all, Alex remained committed to the band and to his brother. Their relationship, though complex, was the bedrock of everything they achieved. Even as band members came and went, and as the music industry evolved, the bond between Alex and Eddie remained unbreakable.

The eventual disbandment of Van Halen in 2020, following Eddie's tragic death, was a moment of profound sadness for Alex. It wasn't just the end of a band—it was the loss of his closest companion, the person who had shared every triumph and setback with him. For Alex, continuing without Eddie was unimaginable. The drums that had once echoed with the sounds of their collaboration fell silent, a tribute to a partnership that had defined their lives.

Now, as Alex prepares to share his story with the world through his memoir, Brothers, he does so with a sense of reflection. The book is not just a recounting of Van Halen's rise to fame; it's a personal journey through the highs and lows of his life, offering insights into the unique relationship he shared with Eddie and the incredible journey they took together.

Beyond the music, Alex's life is also a story of resilience. His personal struggles, including hearing loss from years of exposure to loud music, are part of the narrative. But so too are the moments of joy, the friendships forged, and the love he found in his family. His marriages, the birth of his sons Aric and Malcolm, and his role as a father and uncle are chapters that have brought him fulfillment outside of the music world.

Alex's story is also one of giving back. As an ordained minister, he has officiated at the weddings of loved ones, including his brother Eddie's second marriage and the wedding of his ex-sister-in-law Valerie Bertinelli. These moments reflect the importance of family and connection in Alex's life, values that have remained constant even as the world around him changed.

As he looks to the future, Alex Van Halen may no longer be in the spotlight, but his influence continues to resonate. Whether through his upcoming book, his legacy in the music industry, or the wisdom he imparts to the next generation of musicians, Alex's journey is far from over. His story is one of passion, perseverance, and an unbreakable bond with the brother who shared his dreams. And as long as there are drums to beat and songs to be played, the spirit of Van Halen will live on, echoing through the halls of rock history.

As Alex Van Halen settles into this quieter phase of life, his thoughts often turn to the future, not just for himself but for the legacy he and Eddie built together. The release of his memoir, Brothers, is a way to honor that legacy and ensure that the story of Van Halen, in all its complexity, is told through his eyes—unfiltered and genuine.

The book is more than just a recounting of events; it's a reflection on the deeper meaning behind those events. Alex delves into the emotional landscape of their journey, exploring the challenges they faced and the lessons learned along the way. He writes candidly about the tension and friction that sometimes flared within the band, particularly in the dynamic between the Van Halen brothers and the various lead singers who passed through the group. The book also sheds light on the creative process behind their iconic albums, giving fans a glimpse into the meticulous work that went into crafting the sound that defined a generation.

But Brothers is not only about the past. Alex uses the platform to speak to younger musicians, offering advice born from decades in the industry. He emphasizes the importance of staying true to one's artistic vision, the necessity of hard work, and the value of surrounding oneself with people who genuinely care about the music and each other. He also touches on the pitfalls of fame, cautioning against the temptations and distractions that can derail even the most promising careers.

In reflecting on the band's impact, Alex is proud of what they accomplished, but he is also deeply aware of the sacrifices that came with it. The relentless touring schedules, the long hours in the studio, and the constant pressure to outdo themselves took a toll on everyone involved. The memoir serves as both a celebration of their achievements and a sober acknowledgment of the cost of those successes.

Beyond the book, Alex's life continues to be filled with meaningful pursuits. While the drum kit may no longer be the center of his daily routine, music remains a vital part of who he is. He spends time mentoring young drummers, passing on the techniques and philosophies that have shaped his approach to music. His home, once filled with the cacophony of rehearsals and recording sessions, now echoes with the softer, more introspective sounds of his solo playing, as he explores new rhythms and styles that reflect his current state of mind.

Alex also dedicates more time to his family, cherishing the moments with his sons and his extended family. The bonds he has forged over the years, both within and outside the music industry, are more important to him now than ever. He's known for being a devoted father and a supportive presence in the lives of those he cares about, always ready with a word of encouragement or a piece of wisdom.

In his quieter moments, Alex often thinks about Eddie. The loss of his brother is a wound that will never fully heal, but he finds comfort in the memories they shared and the music they created together. He knows that Eddie's spirit lives on in every note, every chord, and every beat of the music they made. And in that music, they are still together, still creating, still pushing the boundaries of what's possible.

Looking forward, Alex envisions a future where the Van Halen legacy continues to inspire. He is involved in discussions about remastering and re-releasing some of the band's classic albums, ensuring that new generations of fans can experience the music in its full glory. He's also exploring the possibility of a documentary or biopic, a project that would allow a deeper dive into the band's history, capturing the essence of what made Van Halen not just a band, but a phenomenon.

As he moves into this next chapter of his life, Alex Van Halen remains a figure of quiet strength and enduring passion. He may no longer be touring the world or headlining massive stadiums, but his influence on the music world is as powerful as ever. Through his memoir, his mentoring, and his ongoing commitment to preserving the Van Halen legacy, Alex continues to shape the world of rock music, ensuring that the beat goes on, even as the lights dim and the curtain falls.

As Alex Van Halen looks to the horizon of his life, he remains deeply rooted in the principles that guided him through decades of musical success and personal trials. The lessons learned in the glare of the spotlight and in the shadows of grief have given him a perspective that he shares freely with those around him. He is not just a legendary drummer; he is a storyteller, a mentor, and a guardian of the legacy that he and Eddie created.

In recent years, Alex has become more involved in philanthropic efforts, using his platform to support causes that resonate with him. He is particularly passionate about music education, believing that every child should have access to the tools and opportunities that allowed him and Eddie to discover their talents. Through donations, fundraising, and personal appearances, Alex works to ensure that the next generation of musicians can find their voice, just as he and his brother did.

The future also holds exciting possibilities for collaborations with artists who were inspired by Van Halen's music. Although he has largely stepped away from public performances, Alex remains open to the idea of special projects that align with his artistic vision. He has been approached by various musicians across different genres, eager to create something that bridges the gap between the past and the present. These collaborations could see Alex returning to the studio, not to recreate the old magic, but to explore new sonic landscapes that honor the spirit of innovation that has always been at the heart of his music.

At home, Alex's life is filled with the warmth and laughter of family. His wife, Stine, and his sons, Aric and Malcolm, are his greatest sources of joy. He finds peace in the simple moments—whether it's watching a sunset, listening to his sons talk about their own passions, or reminiscing with friends over a glass of wine. The pace of life has slowed, but it has also become richer, filled with the appreciation of a man who has lived fully and continues to do so.

As the release date for Brothers approaches, anticipation builds among fans and critics alike. The book is expected to be more than just a memoir; it is a cultural artifact, a deep dive into the heart of one of rock's most enduring bands. The promotional tour, while not as grueling as the endless cycles of Van Halen's heyday, will give Alex the opportunity to connect with fans in a more intimate setting. Book signings, interviews, and speaking engagements will allow him to share his story directly with those who have followed his career from the beginning.

Looking ahead, Alex sees his role not just as a keeper of the Van Halen flame, but as an elder statesman of rock. He's been approached by several organizations and institutions to lend his expertise and experience to initiatives aimed at preserving the history of rock music. Whether through museum exhibitions, educational programs, or advisory roles, Alex is eager to contribute to the ongoing celebration of the genre that defined his life.

In the quiet moments, when he's alone with his thoughts, Alex reflects on the extraordinary journey he's had. From a young boy in Nijmegen, dreaming of a life filled with music, to the heights of rock stardom, to the challenges and losses that inevitably come with time, it has been a life well-lived. And while the roar of the crowd may have faded, the music still plays on in his heart, a constant reminder of the brotherhood, the creativity, and the love that fueled Van Halen's rise to greatness.

As Alex Van Halen continues down this path, one thing is certain: the story of Van Halen is far from over. It lives on in every beat of the drum, every strum of the guitar, and every fan who finds something in their music that speaks to them. And as long as that music is played, the legacy of the Van Halen brothers will endure, a testament to the power of rock and the bonds of family.

Even as Alex Van Halen settles into a life of quieter reflection, his influence continues to ripple through the world of rock and beyond. The release of his book Brothers in October 2024 marks not just a culmination of his journey but also an invitation to fans and historians alike to delve into the intricate dynamics of one of the most iconic bands in history. Through the pages, readers will find a story of ambition, creativity, and the deep familial bond that both strengthened and tested the Van Halen brothers over the years.

In the months following the book's release, Alex embarks on a promotional tour that takes him across the United States and Europe. The tour is a blend of intimate book signings and larger speaking engagements where Alex shares anecdotes and insights into the making of Van Halen's music, the challenges of fame, and the personal sacrifices that came with it. Fans are eager to hear his perspective, particularly as he opens up about his relationship with Eddie—how they inspired each other, how they fought, and ultimately, how they remained inseparable, both musically and emotionally, until Eddie's passing in 2020.

During these events, Alex also discusses his decision to auction off his drum gear, a move that many saw as the symbolic closing of a chapter in his life. He speaks candidly about the reasons behind it, explaining that the auction was less about letting go and more about moving forward. "It was time," he says. "Time to share those pieces with the world, with fans who cherished the music we made. Those drums—they're part of the story, but they're not the end of it."

The drum auction, held in June 2024, turns out to be one of the largest and most anticipated events of its kind. Collectors and fans from around the globe bid on items that span Alex's entire career—from his first Ludwig drum kit used during the recording of Van Halen to the massive, custom-built sets that became a signature of his later tours. The proceeds from the auction are donated to music education programs and hearing loss research, causes that are close to Alex's heart. He hopes that these contributions will help inspire the next generation of musicians and provide support for those who have, like him, suffered from the physical tolls of a life in rock and roll.

Meanwhile, Alex remains deeply involved in the preservation of Van Halen's legacy. Collaborating with music historians, he works on curating an extensive archive of the band's work, including unreleased tracks, rare footage, and personal artifacts. This archive is intended not only for a future museum exhibition but also as a resource for documentaries and academic research on the evolution of rock music. Alex's commitment to this project ensures that the essence of Van Halen will be preserved for future generations to explore and appreciate.

In his personal life, Alex continues to find joy in the simple pleasures that come with being surrounded by family. His sons, Aric and Malcolm, are now grown, with Aric pursuing his passion for athletics and Malcolm exploring his own creative endeavors. Alex takes pride in their achievements, often reflecting on how his own journey influenced their paths. His relationship with his wife, Stine, remains a cornerstone of his life, providing him with the stability and love that carried him through the highs and lows of his career.

As the years go by, Alex occasionally entertains the idea of returning to the studio, not for a full-fledged comeback, but for the sheer joy of creating music again. He's been in touch with a few old friends and collaborators, exploring the possibility of working on a project that honors the spirit of experimentation that characterized Van Halen's music. Whether or not this project comes to fruition, the idea itself keeps his creative spark alive.

Ultimately, Alex Van Halen's story is one of resilience, passion, and the enduring power of music. Though the chapter of Van Halen as a band has closed, the legacy lives on, carried forward by the millions of fans who found their own lives changed by the music he and Eddie created. As Alex steps back from the public eye, he does so with a sense of fulfillment, knowing that he has contributed something timeless to the world.

And so, as he looks back on a life filled with extraordinary accomplishments, Alex Van Halen can rest assured that his place in the annals of rock history is secure. His drumming, his innovations, and his dedication to the craft have left an indelible mark on music. And in every beat, every echo of those unforgettable drum solos, the spirit of Van Halen lives on, forever a testament to the magic that happens when passion, talent, and brotherhood come together in perfect harmony.

As the years pass, Alex Van Halen continues to navigate the balance between his enduring legacy and the quieter life he has embraced. While the music industry evolves and new generations of artists emerge, Alex's influence remains palpable, inspiring countless drummers and musicians who cite him as a key influence in their own careers. His distinct drumming style, characterized by powerful rhythms and intricate patterns, has become a blueprint for aspiring rock musicians around the world.

The book Brothers becomes a bestseller, resonating with both fans and critics alike. Readers appreciate Alex's honesty, his willingness to reveal the complexities of his relationship with Eddie, and the behind-the-scenes stories that shaped the band's trajectory. The book not only offers a glimpse into the world of Van Halen but also serves as a broader reflection on the nature of fame, creativity, and the bonds that hold families together. It earns accolades, including a nomination for a prestigious literary award, cementing Alex's status not just as a legendary musician, but also as a storyteller with a unique voice.

In the aftermath of the book's success, Alex receives numerous invitations to participate in documentaries, interviews, and podcasts. He carefully selects his appearances, preferring to engage in projects that offer a deep, respectful exploration of Van Halen's impact on music history. One such project is a comprehensive documentary series produced by a major streaming service, which delves into the rise of hard rock and heavy metal in the late 20th century. Alex plays a significant role in the series, providing insights and anecdotes that give viewers a richer understanding of the era.

Despite his semi-retirement from the public eye, Alex remains a sought-after figure in the music world. He is frequently asked to mentor young drummers, participate in charity events, and even guest-appear on albums. Although he turns down most offers, preferring to stay true to his decision to step back, there are occasional exceptions—moments when he feels compelled to share his wisdom and experience with those who seek it.

One such exception occurs in 2026 when a group of young, talented musicians approaches Alex with a proposal for a collaborative project. They are deeply inspired by Van Halen's music and want to create a tribute album that reinterprets some of the band's classic tracks with a modern twist. Intrigued by their passion and impressed by their skills, Alex agrees to contribute, lending his drumming to a few select tracks. The project, released in 2027, is met with critical acclaim and serves as a bridge between the old and new generations of rock music.

Meanwhile, Alex's personal life remains fulfilling. He and Stine continue to enjoy their life together, spending time with their family and traveling when they can. They find solace in nature, often retreating to their home in the hills, where Alex indulges in his love of photography and writing. His sons, Aric and Malcolm, visit frequently, bringing with them the vibrancy of their own pursuits. The family gatherings are filled with laughter, music, and the stories that only a life as extraordinary as Alex's can generate.

Alex's health, always a concern due to his years of intense drumming and the toll it took on his body, remains stable. He maintains a routine of exercise, meditation, and regular medical check-ups, all of which help him manage the physical challenges of aging. His hearing, severely affected by decades of exposure to loud music, is carefully monitored, and he continues to advocate for hearing protection in the music industry, using his platform to raise awareness about the importance of safeguarding musicians' health.

As the 2030s approach, Alex reflects on the possibility of writing a follow-up to Brothers—a book that would focus more on his personal journey, the lessons he has learned, and the wisdom he wishes to impart to future generations. He begins drafting chapters, drawing from the rich tapestry of his life experiences. This new book, tentatively titled Echoes of the Beat, is a deeply introspective work that delves into his philosophy on life, music, and the importance of staying true to oneself.

While the world continues to evolve and new trends in music come and go, Alex Van Halen's legacy remains a constant—a testament to the enduring power of rock and roll, and the unbreakable bond between two brothers who changed the course of music history. In every corner of the globe, from packed stadiums to small garage bands, the spirit of Van Halen lives on, echoing in the beats of drums, the riffs of guitars, and the hearts of fans who continue to celebrate the music that defined a generation.

And so, as he continues to write his own story in the twilight of his life, Alex Van Halen finds peace in knowing that his journey has been one of purpose, passion, and profound impact. His drums may no longer thunder on stage, but their echoes will resound forever, a reminder of a legacy that transcends time and space, forever etched in the annals of rock history.

As Alex Van Halen moves into the next chapter of his life, his focus shifts toward leaving a lasting impact beyond music. His experiences and reflections on fame, creativity, and the challenges of life in the spotlight inspire him to explore new avenues of influence.

In the late 2030s, Alex becomes involved in various philanthropic endeavors. He establishes the Van Halen Foundation, a charitable organization dedicated to supporting music education and hearing protection for young musicians. Through the foundation, Alex funds scholarships, donates instruments to underprivileged schools, and sponsors programs that teach young artists the importance of preserving their hearing while pursuing their passion for music. The foundation's outreach extends globally, touching the lives of countless aspiring musicians who might otherwise have never had the opportunity to explore their talents.

In addition to his charitable work, Alex becomes a sought-after speaker on the topics of creativity, resilience, and the music industry. He is invited to give keynote addresses at universities, music schools, and industry conferences, where he shares his insights with the next generation of artists and innovators. His speeches are marked by a rare combination of wisdom, humility, and humor, and they resonate deeply with audiences of all ages.

Echoes of the Beat, the book he began drafting in the late 2020s, is finally completed and published in 2034. The book receives widespread acclaim for its candid exploration of Alex's inner world, offering readers a glimpse into the mind of a man who has lived through extraordinary highs and lows. Echoes of the Beat becomes a bestseller, further solidifying Alex's reputation not only as a legendary musician but also as a profound thinker and writer.

As the years progress, Alex remains a guiding force in the lives of his family and friends. He takes pride in watching his sons, Aric and Malcolm, carve out their own paths in life. Aric, who has become a respected coach and mentor in the world of athletics, and Malcolm, who has found success as a musician and producer, both credit their father's unwavering support and wisdom for helping them achieve their goals. Family gatherings continue to be a source of joy for Alex, filled with music, laughter, and the stories that have become a cherished part of the Van Halen legacy.

In 2040, a major retrospective of Van Halen's career is held at the Rock and Roll Hall of Fame. The exhibition, titled Van Halen: The Legacy of Sound, features rare artifacts, interviews, and interactive exhibits that allow fans to experience the band's history in a new and immersive way. Alex plays a key role in curating the exhibit, ensuring that it not only honors the band's musical achievements but also highlights the personal stories behind the music. The exhibit attracts visitors from around the world, further cementing Van Halen's status as one of the most influential rock bands in history.

In the quiet moments of his later years, Alex finds himself drawn back to the drums, not for the stage, but for his own personal fulfillment. He sets up a small drum studio in his home, where he occasionally plays for the sheer joy of it, reconnecting with the instrument that has been such a central part of his life. These private sessions are a source of peace and reflection, a way for Alex to express himself in a language that has always been second nature to him.

As Alex enters his 90s, he is celebrated as a true icon in the world of music, a pioneer whose contributions have shaped the course of rock and roll. His legacy, however, extends far beyond his achievements as a drummer. He is remembered as a man who lived with passion, who embraced both the triumphs and challenges of life with grace, and who used his platform to make a positive difference in the world.

When Alex Van Halen passes away peacefully in 2045, surrounded by his loved ones, the world mourns the loss of a legend. Tributes pour in from all corners of the globe, from fans, fellow musicians, and those who were touched by his music and his generosity. His life is celebrated in a series of concerts, documentaries, and special events that honor not only his musical legacy but also the profound impact he had on the lives of so many.

But even as the world says goodbye, the beat goes on. The rhythms Alex created continue to inspire, his wisdom continues to guide, and his spirit lives on in the hearts of those who loved him and the millions of fans who found meaning in his music. Alex Van Halen's journey may have come to an end, but his legacy—like the sound of his drums—will echo through the ages, a testament to a life well-lived and a story well-told.

In the years following Alex Van Halen's passing, the legacy he left behind only grows more influential. The Van Halen Foundation, which he established during his lifetime, expands its reach, becoming one of the most significant charitable organizations dedicated to music education and hearing protection. The foundation funds numerous initiatives, including the construction of state-of-the-art music schools in underserved communities, and collaborates with leading audiologists to develop innovative hearing protection for musicians.

Alex's book, Echoes of the Beat, remains a timeless classic, studied in music and cultural history courses across the globe. It becomes a touchstone for musicians and creatives who seek to understand the deeper connections between life experiences and artistic expression. The book is often cited as a profound exploration of the human spirit, and its lessons continue to resonate with new generations of artists.

The Rock and Roll Hall of Fame continues to honor Van Halen's contributions to music with an annual event named after Alex: The Van Halen Beat Awards. These awards recognize excellence in drumming and percussion, celebrating both established legends and rising stars in the field. The event becomes a prestigious and eagerly anticipated occasion in the music industry, drawing attention to the art of drumming and ensuring that Alex's influence endures.

In the realm of music, Alex's innovations with drumming techniques and his pioneering use of technology remain a significant part of his legacy. His work is studied and emulated by drummers worldwide, and his unique "brown sound" is often referenced in discussions about the evolution of rock music. The signature instruments and equipment that Alex developed continue to be popular among musicians, and his influence can be heard in the work of countless artists across various genres.

Malcolm Van Halen, Alex's younger son, carries on the musical tradition, becoming a highly respected producer and musician in his own right. He often speaks of the wisdom and guidance his father provided, and he dedicates much of his work to preserving the Van Halen legacy. Malcolm also takes an active role in the Van Halen Foundation, ensuring that the organization continues to thrive and expand its mission.

In a poignant tribute to his father, Malcolm organizes a series of tribute concerts that feature some of the biggest names in music, all paying homage to Alex and the band that defined a generation. These concerts are not only a celebration of the music but also a fundraiser for the Van Halen Foundation, ensuring that Alex's legacy of giving back continues for many years to come.

Aric Van Halen, Alex's elder son, continues to excel in the world of athletics, but he also finds ways to honor his father's memory. He becomes involved in efforts to raise awareness about the importance of hearing protection, particularly for athletes who are exposed to loud environments. Aric's advocacy work brings attention to a cause that was close to his father's heart, and he helps develop new technologies that protect hearing without compromising performance.

The Van Halen family remains a tight-knit unit, bonded not only by their shared history but also by their commitment to carrying forward Alex's values and vision. They gather regularly to celebrate milestones and to remember the man who, despite his fame and success, always put family first.

As the decades pass, Alex Van Halen's name becomes synonymous with not just great music, but also with integrity, innovation, and a deep commitment to making the world a better place. His life story is told and retold in documentaries, biographies, and academic studies, each one highlighting different facets of his extraordinary journey.

In the end, Alex Van Halen's legacy is about more than just the music he created. It is about the way he lived his life—with passion, creativity, and a dedication to helping others. It is about the people he inspired, the innovations he pioneered, and the positive impact he made on the world.

Alex Van Halen's story is one of triumph and resilience, of a man who followed his own path and, in doing so, left an indelible mark on the world. His spirit lives on in every beat of the drums, every note of the music, and every life he touched. And as long as there are people who love music, who believe in the power of creativity, and who strive to make a difference, the legacy of Alex Van Halen will continue to inspire and endure.

Made in the USA
Coppell, TX
02 December 2024